MINDFORCE

MINDFORCE

HAS BEEN SPECIALLY WRITTEN FOR TESCO BY
GUY LYON-PLAYFAIR

Published for
Tesco Stores Limited
by Brilliant Books Ltd
84-86 Regent Street
London W1R 5PA

First published 1999

Text and Illustrations © 1999 Brilliant Books Ltd
Printed by Poligrafico Dehoniano, Italy
Reproduction by Colourpath, London

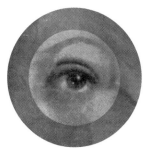

MINDFORCE

GUY LYON-PLAYFAIR

ACKNOWLEDGEMENTS

Fortean Picture Library: p31

George Todd: p61

Guy Lyon-Playfair: p16, p38

Mary Evans Picture Library: p9, p30, p60

Mary Evans Picture Library: p15, p45, p58, p78, p82 (Guy Lyon-Playfair)

Mary Evans Picture Library/Harry Price College,

Univ. of London: p75 (Peter Underwood)

Mary Evans/Society for Psychical Research: p41

Thelma Moss/Playfair Archive: p64

COVER ILLUSTRATION BY MATTHEW COOPER

CONTENTS

MINDFORCE
INTRODUCTION

"THE PARANORMAL IS BUNK.
THOSE WHO TRY TO SELL IT TO US ARE
FAKES AND CHARLATANS."

The statement above was made in 1998 by Richard Dawkins of the Committee for the Public Understanding of Science. He informed the supposedly ignorant public that "to call something paranormal means it is forever impossible for science to explain". That is not how my dictionary chooses to define 'paranormal' – it describes it as "beyond the range of normal experience or scientific explanation". It certainly does not use the word 'forever'. With all the incredible discoveries science makes every year, how can anyone predict what secrets will be unlocked in the next ten years, let alone in the next hundred?

Sceptics who believe that the 'paranormal' is bunk should be reminded of what was described as bunk at the turn of the last century, by one of the most respected scientists of his time, Lord Kelvin. He said the whole idea of alternating current, the form of electricity every home now uses, was a "gigantic mistake". He thought that "X-rays will prove to be a hoax". He also declared he had no faith at all in any form of flight other than ballooning.

PERPETUAL MIRACLE

Sir Isaac Newton, generally seen as the first and greatest modern scientist, took a very different approach to the unknown. He is remembered for his pioneering discovery of gravity – but freely admitted that he could not explain it completely. Indeed, he called gravity a "perpetual miracle". When a colleague objected to such unscientific language, Newton insisted that mankind should learn from "phenomena of nature", even if their cause was as yet unknown.

Even today, we still know little more about gravity than Newton did, yet we cannot deny that it exists. It is literally all around us, as are many other strange things that we cannot explain. Some of these may turn out to be 'bunk' – others may not. To decide in advance what can or can't be true is hardly a scientific approach.

This book does not promise a set of glib answers to all the deepest mysteries of human life. It will, however, examine the latest theories surrounding those "phenomena of nature" which we have no shortage of evidence for, but have as yet been unable to explain.

These are often labelled 'paranormal', though I prefer to use the term 'psi', which is commonly used in the field of parapsychology and by most psychical researchers.

My interest in psi is a practical one. Psi phenomena such as telepathy, clairvoyance, precognition, psychokinesis and especially non-medical healing have a direct effect on our own lives and can be of great value.

If we can learn to make use of them, we may well be able to understand our world and each other much better than ever before. I have had personal experience of many of the phenomena listed above and offer the best evidence I have discovered for the rest.

I will not be covering certain subjects that often tend to get lumped in with the paranormal – including crop circles, the Bermuda Triangle, and pyramid power. This does not mean I consider them 'bunk'. In fact, one or two of them I consider to have been proved to exist. Crop circles, for example, do exist – a new one pops up every day like a giant mushroom, it seems, and some of them are splendid works of art. However, many are known to have been made by human artists, and in the absence of any real evidence to the contrary, I suspect that all of them may have been.

MYSTERIES

As for Bigfoot, Nessie and the Abominable Snowperson (or yeti), I am far from satisfied that any of them exists, though

MYSTERY LADY: *One of the few photographs of a ghost that has never been explained is this picture taken in 1936 at Raynham Hall, Norfolk. Could it be reflected light? A chemical stain on the negative? Or was the mystery lady of Raynham Hall really caught on film, going up the stairs?*

I am quite prepared to change my mind if the evidence for any of them gets better.

The Bermuda Triangle, in which ships and aircraft have been vanishing for centuries, is an enigma which has created a whole industry of its own. Yet only recently a normal explanation, supported by plenty of evidence, has been put forward, although many are still unaware of it. It seems that earthquakes under the sea can release gases which ionise the air above and knock out aircraft instruments. These gases also alter the specific gravity of the sea, which can actually cause ships to sink. This has been so convincingly demonstrated with a model ship in a tank, that I for one, am satisfied this famous mystery has finally been solved.

All the subjects in this book are definitely examples of what Newton called "phenomena of nature" – and they do indeed appear to require study. Explanations will have to wait, and they will not come without investigation. It took scientists about a hundred years to find out exactly how aspirin works – yet that didn't stop it from working. As for gravity, we still cannot explain it.

Robert Youngson, in his book Scientific Blunders, published in 1998, tells us: "The whole history of science, right up to the present, is a story of refusal to accept fundamental new ideas; of older people of scientific eminence dying in confirmed possession of their lifelong beliefs; and of painful readjustment of younger people to new concepts."

If you are prepared for some readjustment of your belief system – and it needn't be all that painful – open your mind and come inside.

The truth is not 'out there' but in here. Read on!

TELEPATHY HAPPENS

"JACK WAS PULLED OUT — BADLY INJURED, BUT STILL ALIVE. SAVED BY WHAT WE CAN ONLY CALL A TELEPATHIC SOS MESSAGE."

Don't try to tell Jack Sullivan there's no such thing as telepathy. He knows it saved his life. Late one afternoon he was alone in a trench 14 feet deep, welding a line of new water pipes in Washington Street, Boston, USA. He had just stopped some children from playing around by his truck because he was concerned for their safety. He pulled his welding mask down, ready for a final hour of work, grateful that he would soon be packing up and heading back home. Then, silently and without warning, the whole trench caved in on top of him. Later he recalled: "Tons of dirt hit me from above and behind. It knocked me down against the pipe, jamming my shoulder up against the red-hot weld. My legs were doubled up under me, my head had hit the pipe and my nose was smashed against the shield."

Helpless, he tried to cry out, but there was nobody around, and his noisy generator was still running. He thought he was going to die.

Running out of oxygen, and in terrible pain, his thoughts turned to his wife and his five

11

children. He thought of each one in succession, conjuring them up in his mind as clearly as if they had all been standing there right beside him.

Then, for reasons he was never able to explain, his mind started to focus on someone quite unexpected – one of his fellow workmates.

Street project had not been touched for the last two weeks.

Despite having to drive several miles through heavy traffic he was in the habit of avoiding, a nagging feeling inexplicably drew him to the site.

As soon as he got there he spotted the generator with its cable leading straight to the

For reasons he was never able to explain, his mind started to focus on someone quite unexpected – one of his fellow workmates...

Tommy Whittaker was working in another part of town and did not even know where Jack was. And he too had a sudden impulse he could not account for. He felt he had to go over to the Washington Street site and check that everything was all right. He had an uneasy feeling that it wasn't – even though he had no reason to think that anyone was working there. In fact, he knew that the Washington

cave-in. The next thing he saw was Jack's hand, which in desperation he had just managed to raise to the surface. About two hours after the disaster had struck, Jack was pulled out – badly injured but still alive. Saved by what we can only call a telepathic SOS message.

There are plenty more cases like this, if somewhat less dramatic. A typical one involved the great German conductor

Bruno Walter, who was taken ill at a dinner party while he was on tour. His host called a taxi to take him back to his hotel, but it did not arrive, so Walter went to look for another one. Out in the street, he immediately saw his manager driving past and waved at him to stop.

What a timely coincidence, said Walter, that he happened to be passing by. His manager replied that it was not a coincidence – he had just had 'an intense feeling' that Walter was in trouble and had driven off to look for him.

This account was given by Walter to his friend, American writer and social campaigner Upton Sinclair. The author of nearly a hundred plays and novels, Sinclair must have surprised many of his readers when, in 1930, he produced a detailed study of telepathy in a book which he called Mental Radio. It contained a preface by Albert Einstein, no less, and is still one of the best books on the subject. It includes an account of a long series of experiments in mental communication carried out in Sinclair's own home with his wife Mary Craig Sinclair as the receiver and Upton himself taking on the task of the sender.

HISTORIC EXPERIMENTS

For them, it was a kind of parlour game in which Upton would do a simple drawing while Mary Craig, in another room behind a closed door, would draw what she 'saw'.

They kept it up for about a year and did a total of 290 tests, in which Sinclair reckoned that his wife was totally successful for 23 per cent of the time, partially successful for 53 per cent, and unsuccessful for only 24 per cent. In other words, she got three times as many right or nearly right as she got wrong.

MENTAL RADIO

Some of her hits were right on target. Upton Sinclair went in for plain speaking, and he had these words to say about the historic experiments in which he had participated: "I tell you – and because it is so important, I put it in capital letters:

"TELEPATHY HAPPENS!"

The Sinclair experiments did indeed make history. One man who was particularly impressed by them was psychologist Dr William McDougall, a former head of the psychology department at Oxford University who went on to hold the same post at Harvard. As soon as he had read Mental Radio, he went to visit the Sinclairs with the aim of doing some experiments himself. Mary Craig did not particularly like the idea of being tested, but reluctantly agreed to do what she could. The professor told her he had

a picture in his pocket. Could she describe it? Mrs Sinclair sat down, closed her eyes and said she saw "a building with stone walls and narrow windows … covered with green leaves". McDougall produced his picture – of the ivy-clad walls of an Oxford college.

McDougall was just about to take up his new job at Duke University in Durham, North Carolina. He promised the Sinclairs that the first thing he would do would be to found a department for scientifically conducted psychical research. So he did, and a new scientific discipline, that of parapsychology, came into being in 1927.

The professor was succeeded by his students Joseph Banks Rhine and Louisa Rhine, who were to become the most well-known psi-researchers of their generation. It is largely because of their dedicated efforts that the field of parapsychology is now accepted as a serious science throughout the world.

At Duke University, the emphasis was on laboratory experiments usually involving long (and boring) runs of card-guessing and coin tossing. Tedious as these were, they clearly showed that something other than chance was at work.

The same can be said for the more recent experiments similar to the Sinclairs', which use film clips instead of simple drawings. Again, successful results occur overwhelmingly against chance.

PERCHANCE TO DREAM...

One of the most successful experiments in telepathy of all time took place in 1971, when a young Englishman named Malcolm Bessent went to the Maimonides Medical Centre in New York, lay on a bed and promptly went to sleep. There was absolutely nothing wrong with him – the reason he was there was to put to the test his reputation as one of the most outstanding receivers of tele-pathic impressions.

MALCOLM BESSENT: *A psychic with the power to pick up the thoughts of others – while dreaming.*

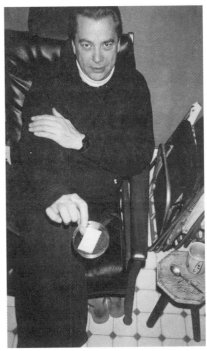

Forty-five miles away, the pop group The Grateful Dead were giving a concert to an audience of 2,000. At 11.30pm the crowd were told that they were about to take part in a live test. A slide would be shown on the screen, and they would try to 'send' it

In New York, the laboratory assistant noticed that Malcolm had reached the 'rapid eye movement' stage of sleep, indicating that he was dreaming. Once his eye movements had stopped, she woke him, and then asked him to describe his

ZENER CARDS: *have distinctive symbolic signs, used for experiments in telepathy.*

to Malcolm so he could dream about it. The slide, chosen at random, was The Seven Spinal Chakras– a mystical painting of a man meditating. His seven chakras or 'energy centres' on his spinal column were picked out in strong colours and his head had a bright sun-like halo.

dreams. This is what he said: "I was interested in using natural energy. I was talking to this guy who said he'd invented a way of using solar energy and he showed me this box ... He was suspended in mid-air or something ... I'm remembering a dream I had about an energy

16

box and a spinal column." Was it a coincidence? A lucky guess? Maybe not, for the experiment was held on each of the six evenings when The Grateful Dead performed at the Capitol Theatre in Port Chester, and Malcolm scored what was independently judged to be a direct hit four times out of six. An interesting feature of his chakra dream is the roundabout way he approached the target before mentioning "an energy box and a spinal column".

was not only being tested for telepathy but also precognition. The target slide sequence was only selected after he had woken up and recorded all his dreams for the night. He had four in total, and two were all about birds. The slides the viewer then looked at were of birds of all shapes and sizes – and nothing else.

Altogether, Malcolm Bessent took part in 16 such dream experiments, scoring a direct hit no less than 14 times.

"Birds – I just have a feeling that the next target material will be about birds."

On other occasions he was much more specific. In an experiment held with just one sender instead of 2,000, his dream report ended: "Birds – I just have a feeling that the next target material will be about birds." What was unusual about this experiment was that he

In 1997, he was persuaded to do another dream telepathy experiment for The Paranormal World of Paul McKenna series on Carlton TV. Again he was completely successful. His sudden death at the age of 53, a few weeks after the film was shown, robbed researchers of one of the most reliable and cooperative subjects they had ever known. He will be remembered for helping to prove that it really is possible to demonstrate telepathy in controlled laboratory conditions.

THE TWIN LINK

Telepathy only happens rarely between total strangers. It is far more likely to occur between relatives and close friends, or people who at least have some connection with each other.

Nobody can be closer to each other than identical twins – since they grow from the same fertilised egg and have the same genes, they are basically the same person. So we might reasonably expect them to share telepathic thoughts more often than non-twins.

Take the case of Mrs Anna Powles from Nottinghamshire. Like Jack Sullivan, she also believes that telepathy has saved a life. When her boys were only a few days old, she was feeding them one evening when the one she was holding suddenly started to scream and shake all over.

Mrs Powles had the presence of mind to suspect at once that he was picking up a distress signal from his brother, and it seems he was. The other baby had turned over, buried his head in a pillow and turned blue in the face. He was in the process of suffocating to death.

He was rushed to hospital and luckily survived. "Without a doubt," Mrs Powles told me, "Ricky saved his brother's life." I think she also deserves some of the credit, and this dramatic case suggests that telepathy should be taken more seriously.

Another case from my own collection (published here for the first time, as is the case above) involved a curious coincidence. When the publisher

Ross McWhirter was shot dead in his North London home in 1975, it occurred to me at the time that some valuable scientific data might emerge from this appalling affair. Did his twin brother Norris react, I wondered? I did not know him, and did not think it tactful to write to him. I read the book he wrote in memory of his brother, and found no mention of telepathy in it, so I thought maybe he had not reacted. I was wrong. Just after agreeing to write this book, I learned that the publisher was Norris McWhirter's son, and at our first meeting he spontaneously told me what had happened:

"We were getting ready to go to my sister's school play, and I was standing in the drawing room with my father. Suddenly, for no apparent reason, he slumped down into a chair. He looked dazed. I was terrified and thought he had suffered a heart attack. A few minutes after he recovered, the phone rang and it was the police ..."

After the incident, Norris remembered nothing at all about it. But it had occurred at exactly the moment of his brother's murder.

HOW DOES IT HAPPEN?

The short answer is that we don't know how telepathy happens. Yet perhaps our most important clue is to be found in the Sullivan/Whittaker case which began this chapter.

When the trench fell in on Sullivan, we can be sure that he was in a state of extreme nervous stimulation such as we experience when our adrenalin is flowing, especially at times of severe stress or danger.

Tommy Whittaker, however, performing the monotonous task of welding, was in just the opposite condition – when the nervous system calms us down by slowing the heartbeat, and lowering blood pressure. This can relax us to the point where we are virtually in a trance, and are prone to daydreaming – or receiving a telepathic message.

Generally speaking then, a sender of telepathy has to be in a stimulated state, and the receiver must be in a relaxed, almost vacant condition.

As for how telepathy happens, we have fewer clues. One of the first to tackle this problem seriously was the maverick American scientist Dr Andrija Puharich, who is best known for discovering Uri Geller.

He explained in some detail how theories of 'mental radio' simply would not do for a number of reasons, chiefly because there is no evidence that telepathy grows weaker over distance – or indeed time. However, he pointed out that there is a force of nature that can operate relatively undiminished over huge distances – the power of gravity.

"The sender does not send anything out," he said, "but rather serves as a centre of attraction, drawing to him the attention of the receiver." If this is so, we may not have a full explanation of telepathy for some time, since even after centuries of human curiosity we still do not have one for gravity. We believe we know what it is and what it does, and the same goes for telepathy.

One thing we can say for certain: telepathy cannot be fully explained in terms of physics, biology or psychology as they are presently understood. This is mainly why so many scientists claim there's no such thing. Yet there is such a thing, and I suspect that by the end of the 21st century, telepathy will be considered as normal as X-rays and powered flight are today.

YOU CAN SEE FOREVER

TELEPATHY IS MIND-TO-MIND COMMUNICATION, WHEREAS CLAIRVOYANCE IS LITERALLY SEEING THINGS AT A DISTANCE.

The year was 1937 – a Soviet aircraft had disappeared after flying over the North Pole, and had come to ground, it was believed – somewhere in Alaska – an area six times larger than the UK. The Arctic explorer Sir Hubert Wilkins was asked to go and look for it, and after first searching the area in a Flying Boat – without success – the Soviet Government asked him to try again and mount a full-scale search and rescue mission.

Before he set out with his crew in their Lockheed Electra, Wilkins happened to be chatting with a fellow member of his New York club, a writer named Harold Sherman. The two men found that they shared an interest in psychic matters. Sherman possessed considerable experience of clairvoyance and telepathy and took the existence of both for granted.

Telepathy, as must be clearly indicated, is mind-to-mind communication, whereas clairvoyance is literally seeing things at a distance.

Wilkins happened to say that he was expecting radio difficulties on his trip because of magnetic disturbance caused by high sunspot activity. There would almost certainly be periods in which he would be unable to communicate in any way with his New York base – any normal way, that is.

TUNING IN

Sherman had an idea. This would be a perfect opportunity to put his psi abilities to the test. Could psychic communication succeed where radio failed? He suggested that he would spend half an hour on three evenings a week 'tuning in' to Wilkins and writing down his impressions, to be compared eventually with the log that Wilkins would keep.

The explorer liked the idea, having had experience of this kind of communication among the Aborigines in his native Australia. He set off on 25 October 1937 and, over the next five months, he and Sherman took part in what is

probably the longest and most successful psi experiment of any kind on record. Sherman produced a total of 68 separate reports, containing about 300 specific statements. Not surprisingly, the majority of these referred to snow, ice and cold. Yet many were about quite unlikely incidents that could hardly have been predicted. One evening, he wrote this:

"You in company, men in military attire, some women, evening dress, important people present, much conversation. You appear to be in evening dress yourself."

One would not expect an Arctic explorer to wear evening dress, but this is just what Wilkins was doing at the time. He had been unexpectedly invited to an Armistice Ball in the Alaskan town of Regina. It was attended by local military top brass, and he had to borrow an evening suit for the occasion. A few days later, Sherman again picked up "some kind of banquet, seem to see it held in church". He added, "connection school, standing front of blackboard chalk in hand, you give short talk."

That evening, Wilkins was attending a banquet held at Missionary's House in Point Barrow in the far north of some visitors about diamond mines he had visited in Africa. Sherman correctly identified almost the precise moment when Wilkins reluctantly had to abandon his search, and predicted the day he would return home to New York.

The overall success rate was phenomenal. "You seem to get all the very strong thoughts and sense the vivid conditions,"

...probably the most successful psi experiment of any kind on record...

Alaska – some 4,000 miles from New York – and that same morning he had given a talk to the local schoolchildren.

Other correct impressions were of a fire, a funeral, a ladder, a toothache and a diamond mine. On the days in question, Wilkins had seen a fire and a funeral, he had needed to use a ladder, he did have toothache and he had been talking to Wilkins reported to Sherman. Amazingly, of the 300 or so statements made, only four or five were definitely wrong.

It is curious to note that one of the least successful experiments involved an attempt to transmit Zener cards – sets of 25 cards first used by J B Rhine at Duke University, consisting of five each of circles, crosses, stars, squares and wavy lines.

Sherman scored slightly above chance, and it may be that Wilkins was not trying very hard. "I was not particularly interested," he admitted later, "in carrying out experiments with these cards because it seemed to me that if there were one especially difficult way to demonstrate the possibility of thought transference, it would be with five marked cards."

Most researchers would agree, and you do not often find Zener cards in psi labs today. Rhine used them because he wanted to find a way in which telepathy or clairvoyance could be assessed statistically. By chance alone, a subject should guess five out of 25 correctly. If somebody consistently gets more than five right, the probability of this being due to chance drops sharply. If somebody gets the whole lot right, as one of Rhine's first subjects did, the probability disappears from sight in a string of zeros. Even so, an analysis carried out at the University of Edinburgh, where Britain's first professorship in parapsychology was set up under the terms of the will of writer Arthur Koestler, revealed that when the results of all ESP experiments were added up, the probability of their successes being due to chance was one to ten million. Most people would accept that as convincing proof.

PSI SPIES

Telepathy and clairvoyance undoubtedly happen, but can they be put to practical use? They can, and have been.

In 1972, an unusual series of clairvoyance experiments got under way as a result of a chance meeting between scientist Dr Harold Puthoff, New York artist and writer Ingo Swann and retired police commissioner Pat Price. Swann had already done several highly successful psi experiments, while Price had been using his abilities in his detective work for years. Puthoff worked as a physicist specialising in lasers at what has now become SRI International, a major high-tech think-tank in a suburb of San Francisco. With his fellow laser physicist Russell Targ, he began experiments in what they called Remote Viewing. The sender goes to a randomly selected site and takes in whatever view he finds there. The receiver sits in the SRI office with one of the experimenters and simply describes whatever comes to mind. Pat Price scored a direct hit on his first attempt. Puthoff drove to a site, which could have been absolutely anything in the area, and found himself looking straight at the Hoover Tower on the Stanford University campus. Pat Price's recorded impressions actually included the telling phrase: "seems like it would have to be the Hoover Tower."

MAP READER

Swann was equally successful, and it was he who suggested taking things a stage further. There was no need for anyone to go anywhere, he said. All he needed was a map coordinate, in the form of the exact longitude and latitude. So the researchers asked a colleague who knew nothing about their work to provide them with a list of ten coordinates. Swann just described what he could see at, for example, 60 degrees north, and 19 degrees west. "Volcano to southwest. I think I'm over ocean." The figures were for a location close to the Mount Hekla volcano in Iceland. Swann was found to be correct seven times out of ten, inconclusive twice and definitely wrong only once.

A few weeks after the Remote Viewing programme got under way, a couple of men from the CIA turned up, showing much interest and waving a cheque book. Thus, as was officially admitted in 1995, the whole thing was funded by the Agency, (and later on financed by other agencies).

A good deal of what the remote viewers were up to has yet to be declassified, but it is significant that one of the star performers, Joseph McMoneagle, was awarded the Legion of Merit in 1984. Revealingly, his information they produced was confirmed two weeks later by the Mariner 10 space probe.

The CIA turned up, showing much interest and waving a cheque book...

No wonder they were interested – Swann and Price showed that they could remote view just about anything, anywhere. Price even produced an astonishingly accurate description of a Soviet nuclear plant that included details that were only verified later.

The most bizarre experiment involved Swann leaving Earth altogether and taking a look at Mercury in a joint project with Harold Sherman. Much of the citation described him as "one of the original planners and movers of a unique intelligence project that is revolutionising the intelligence community." His efforts were described as producing "crucial and vital intelligence unavailable from any other source".

At least one of the project's greatest successes was made public, and by no less a person than President Carter. In 1978, a Soviet Tupolev-22 spy plane went missing over Zaire and was assumed to have crashed. The CIA wanted to get hold of it before the Soviets did, and sent urgent faxes to remote viewers in California and at an air force base in Ohio where another team had been put together. Two viewers gave very similar accounts of their impressions, and it was as a result of these that a CIA search party found the plane. President Carter described what the viewer had done: "She went into a trance and, while she was in the trance, gave some latitude and longitude figures. We focused our satellite cameras on that point and the plane was there."

The other viewer, an SRI staff member named Gary Langford, drew a picture of the Tupolev's tail sticking out of a brown river. When the search party reached the site, this was exactly as the plane was found.

It is hard to imagine, somehow, that the remote viewing programme has ceased, as is now officially claimed. It is equally unlikely that we will be hearing much more about it, at least for the time being.

FINDING THE BODY

Several US military remote viewers have left the service and set up private companies. It is not surprising that their clients tend to want to remain anonymous. For some strange reason, people have no qualms about using psychics to their advantage, but they don't want anybody to know about it.

There have been exceptions. Police officer Dennis Naggy from Carteret, New Jersey, has admitted that he called on retired army remote viewer David Morehouse to help find a body, which was fished out of a river just 300 yards from where Morehouse said it was.

Lee Rumbell, an officer with the Royal Canadian Mounted Police, worked for many years with the clairvoyant Maureen McGuire, and told me personally that she helped to lead a search plane to the site of a helicopter crash in the mountains.

At least one case is on record where a man has been sent to prison, following evidence obtained with the help of a clairvoyant. In 1990 D Scott Rogo, a prolific author and prominent member of the Parapsychological Association, was found murdered in his home near Los Angeles. A suspect, John Battista, was detained for questioning, but released. Then Betty Bandy, a close friend of Rogo's, assembled a team of clairvoyants and built up a picture of the man they believed had committed the murder. One of the team, Armand Marcotte, insisted that the killer had left a fingerprint on a glass at the scene. But the police had already found the glass and the print, and had been unable to match it to Battista's. "It's kind of eerie," the detective in charge of the case told the Los Angeles Daily News. "We re-ran the prints after this guy said it. It came back a positive make on Battista." In 1991, Battista was found guilty of Rogo's murder and given 15 years to life.

SO WHY AREN'T YOU RICH?

"If you're so psychic then why aren't you a millionaire yet?" There are several answers to this question often asked of people with psi abilities. Some are not rich because they prefer not to charge for their services. There are others, however, who have done very well for themselves – there is at least one psi millionaire, whom we will meet in a later chapter.

SEEING IT COMING

"I DREAMT I WENT TO SCHOOL AND
THERE WAS NO SCHOOL THERE."
ERIN JONES, AGED TEN, ABERFAN, OCTOBER 1966.

One day in October 1966, ten-year-old Erin Jones abruptly announced to her mother: "Mummy, I'm afraid to die!" According to a statement, later signed by Erin's parents, her astonished mother said, "Why do you talk of dying, and you so young; do you want a lollipop?" "No, but I shall be with Peter and June," Erin went on, referring to two friends at Pantglas School, Aberfan.

Two weeks later, on 20 October, Erin again surprised her mother. "Let me tell you about my dream last night!" Mrs Jones said she was too busy to give her any attention. But Erin insisted, "No Mummy, you must listen." Her mother stopped what she was doing and the little girl went on to tell her, "I dreamt I went to school and there was no school there. Something black had come down all over it."

The next day she went to school as usual – for the last time. At 9.15am a huge pile of coal above the school became a lethal landslide. Soon there was no school to be seen, and 128 children, plus 16 adults, lay dead, buried in the rubble.

It was one of the worst disasters in British history, and little Erin was not the only one who seemed to see it coming. Dr JC Barker, a consultant psychiatrist from Shrewsbury, visited Aberfan soon after the tragedy and was struck by the number of accounts he was given of premonitions similar to Erin's. As the result of an appeal in the press, he received a total of 76 letters, of which 36 involved dreams. They came from all over the country.

Two dreamers actually mentioned Aberfan by name. And a woman from Sheffield had a vision just before the event, of children going to heaven, in Welsh national costume.

NOSTRADAMUS: *(Right)*
THE PROPHECIES: *(Far right)*
Title page of the 1668 edition showing two events he predicted – the death of Henry II and the Great Fire of London.

FROM NOSTRADAMUS TO DUNNE

Critics complain that since we all dream several times every night, we are bound to have a dream sooner or later that corresponds with something that happened either before or after it. If I dream about a black cat, for instance, and see a black cat along my garden wall, I am not particularly surprised because such a cat walks along it nearly every day. But if someone like Erin Jones has a very clear dream about something wholly

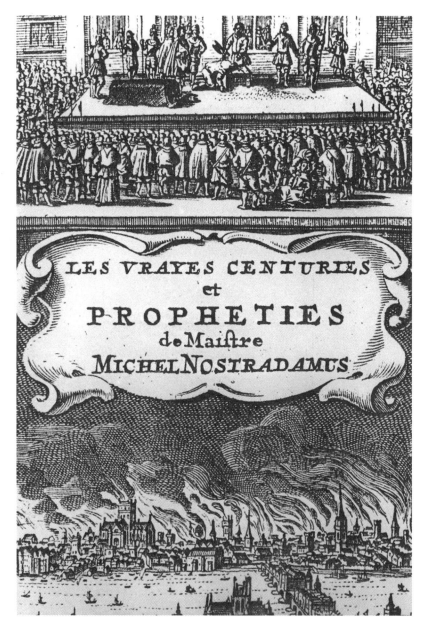

LES VRAYES CENTURIES
et
PROPHETIES
de Maistre
MICHEL NOSTRADAMUS

unexpected, that then happens immediately, accompanied by a totally out-of-character remark about being afraid of dying, we can perhaps suspect that we are dealing with precognition.

When we think of precognition, the man whose name springs to mind is the French physician and astrologer Michel de Nôtre Dame (1503–1566), better known as Nostradamus.

NOSTRADAMUS

He published a total of nearly a thousand quatrains, or four-line verses, written in a bewildering mixture of French and several other languages, making full use of anagrams and abbreviations. His first collection came out in 1555 and included the following: "The young lion shall overcome the old man in field of war in a single fight. In cage of gold his eyes will be pierced. Two wounds in one, then die, a cruel death." Four years later, King Henri II was jousting at a tournament with one of his Scots guards, wearing his gold visor, when splinters from his opponent's lance struck him in both his throat and one eye. He died ten days later from blood poisoning – a cruel death indeed.

FORESEEING REVOLUTION

Nostradamus predicted that he would die not in his bed but on the bench beside it, as indeed he did. He was also credited with foreseeing the French Revolution, the rise and fall of Napoleon and even the Second World War. But as Colin Wilson, the paranormal expert, has said: "If the same stanzas can be interpreted as referring to both the sixteenth and twentieth centuries, it may be felt that Nostradamus' prophecies are somewhat lacking in definiteness." This is putting it mildly.

With few exceptions, they are very imprecise. By now, readers will know what to make of one of those exceptions in which "The year 1999, seventh month, [written 'sept mois' – which some believe could refer to September, not July] the great king of terror will descend from the sky."

astrologer or indeed any kind of mystic, but a military officer and pioneer aviator named John William Dunne. He first became fascinated by the subject after noticing that he would frequently have a dream of a very specific incident which would then proceed to happen quite soon afterwards.

Experiences such as this led him to conclude that there was something wrong with our view of time...

Interpreting the quatrains is like taking the Rorschach inkblot test. They offer much weaker evidence for precognition than we have been able to obtain more recently.

NOT A MYSTIC

The man who did more than anybody to make the idea of precognition both acceptable and extremely popular in the twentieth century was not an

Some of these were trivial. For instance, he dreamt that his watch had stopped at half past four, and found when he woke up, that so it had. Another dream was of an unusual combination lock that used letters instead of figures. A few days later, he came across just such a lock. A more dramatic dream was of a massive volcanic eruption and a big newspaper headline, announcing 4,000 casualties.

Later, he opened his paper to read about the eruption in Martinique in which 40,000, not 4,000 had died. He concluded he had dreamt not about the eruption itself, but about the headline, which he had somehow misread.

Experiences such as this led him to conclude that there was something wrong with our view of time, a view shared by one of the most enthusiastic reviewers of his popular book An Experiment in Time, published in 1927. The reviewer was J B Priestley, who was to become one of the most popular novelists and dramatists of his time, three of whose plays were directly inspired by John Dunne's ideas.

Priestley had several dreams similar to Dunne's, and he amassed a large collection of letters from members of the public, following a radio appeal. Studying these, he noted that about half concerned trivia, such as Dunne's watch stopping at 4.30, and the other half involved death and disaster. Yet there seemed to be nothing in between – no dreams about such important things in life as a new job, a future husband or wife, or a new home. It was, he concluded, as if there were two futures, one preordained and the other not. The first could be dreamed about, since it already existed, but the second could not, since it did not exist. So, it seems we do have free will, but only within a predetermined framework.

VIEWING THE FUTURE

Priestley also reckoned that since we are able to view future events, and he was quite convinced that we can, then there must be two of us, as it were – one in the present and one able to move forward or backward in time. These are difficult ideas to grasp, even when expressed by such a skilled writer as J B Priestley. To make any sense, many will feel they should be supported by factual evidence from the laboratory – as indeed they have been.

LOOKING DOWN THE TIME LINE

One of the very first experiments in remote viewing that Pat Price carried out with Harold Puthoff and Russell Targ provided unexpected evidence for something more than simple clairvoyance. It began with the usual routine – Puthoff left the laboratory and set off with no idea where he was going. He drove at random until he came to a spot he thought would make a good target for Price to describe.

Pat Price's description was exceptionally clear. What he saw, was "a little boat jetty" with plenty of small boats around and an oriental-looking building on the waterfront. When Puthoff returned from his excursion, he immediately recognised this as an exact description of where he had just been – the Redwood City Marina, with its jetty, boats and with its pagoda-like roof that did indeed look oriental. This success took on an even greater significance when Puthoff learned the unusual way it had been recorded.

Targ explained. A few minutes after his colleague had left, at 3pm, he had switched on the tape recorder and spoken a brief introduction, mentioning that Puthoff would be at his chosen target site at 3.30. Then Price interrupted him:

"We don't have to wait till then," he said. "I can tell you right now where he will be." It was just a question, apparently, of "looking down the time line". Simple, really.

REMEMBERING THE FUTURE

Price was not the only one who could do this. As mentioned in Chapter 1, Malcolm Bessent could do it in his dreams night after night. So could a team at Princeton University headed by Robert Jahn, of whom we shall hear more in the following chapter. They conducted 227 experiments in looking down the timeline, and the probability of the successes they achieved being attributed to chance was calculated as one in a hundred billion!

Baffling as the idea of looking through time may be for most of us, it does not seem to worry some modern physicists unduly. One of them, Gerald Feinberg, once gave a talk entitled: 'Precognition – a memory of things future'.

Commenting on the Aberfan disaster, he explained that if somebody read a newspaper account of the tragedy, this could have produced "a trace in the brain which went back before it happened" so that the reader "could remember it before it took place".

Another prominent physicist, Richard Feynman, won the Nobel Prize for demonstrating that subatomic particles can move backwards in time. David Bohm, another distinguished physicist and one time collaborator with Einstein, described what he called the Implicate Order, a holographic model of the universe in which past, present and future co-existed in a realm outside of time.

In the final chapter of this book I will be summarising the latest theories of psi. Before then, I hope to describe each of the main areas of life in which it operates. So far, I have only mentioned the mental side of it. Now it is time to move on to the physical side.

ACTION MIND

Psychokinesis, or PK, means movement caused by the mind. As we shall see, there is plenty of it about, and it turns up in some unexpected places. Here's an extract from the motoring magazine Autocar, dated 29 July 1998:

TYRRELL MAGIC

"The Tyrrell mechanics reported a genuine miracle in their pit at Silverstone. Before their very eyes, Uri Geller smoothed his fingers along an eighteen-millimetre combination snap-on spanner and it bent as though it were made of spaghetti."

Uri Geller, of course, has been bending spoons and keys all over the world for more than 30 years. But a spanner? Although I have known Uri well for 15 years, I found this latest exploit exceedingly hard to believe, so I decided to contact the Tyrrell driver Ricardo Rossett at his home in Brazil and asked if he could confirm the remarkable incident.

He could indeed. "Uri came as my guest," he told me, "and bent some spoons for us in the pit. Then one of the mechanics handed him a spanner and asked if he could bend that as well. Uri agreed to try, but he needed a lot of people around. There were about ten of us watching, and it took a while. He held it by one end and rubbed it in the middle, then he took his other hand away and it just bent – upwards."

Now this was a tool made of chrome vanadium, a metal known for its strength and high-temperature stability. It was designed to be completely reliable in the life-or-death world of Formula One engineering, and intended not to bend under any circumstances.

The Tyrrell mechanics tried to straighten it in a vice themselves – and gave up in despair. Geller was given the spanner to add to his collection of memorabilia. I also tried to bend the spanner by force, without the slightest success. Those who still insist that Uri is just a clever magician have some explaining to do.

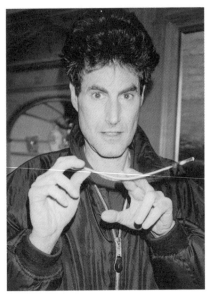

URI GELLER: *With the 18mm chrome vanadium spanner he bent in the Silverstone pits.*

RANDOM EVENT GENERATOR

Current PK research makes much use of various devices known as random event generators, which in theory cannot be affected by people's minds, yet, in practice they are. At Princeton University, aerospace engineer Robert Jahn has installed a kind of huge pinball machine in which 9,000 polystyrene balls are released from the top all at once, finding their way down past 330 pegs and coming to rest in one of 19 bins down at the bottom.

Following the normal process of chance, the balls arrange themselves in a neat bell-curve, with the middle bins nearly full and the outer ones almost empty. The big question is, can 'chance' be influenced?

THE SIMPSON EFFECT

On 3 October 1995, probably the largest-scale psi experiment in history took place in three laboratories simultaneously – including Robert Jahn's at Princeton. At about five o'clock in the evening (GMT) the three random event generators were running normally, the standard results showing up as a more or less straight line moving across their screens.

Then the experimenters at each laboratory switched on their televisions and tuned into the most eagerly awaited event of that year – the verdict in the O J Simpson murder trial.

Then, with an estimated half a billion viewers around the world watching their screens, the 'not guilty' verdict was announced, and the line of dots at the bottom of all five screens suddenly shot up. What this seemed to suggest was that when a large number of people are in an excited state and concentrating on the same thing, some sort of order can be created out of chaos. This has been demonstrated on several other occasions, including during the opening ceremony of the 1996 Olympic Games, when the level of order rose steadily shortly after the opening and stayed well above 'baseline' right up to the end of the five-hour broadcast.

The implications of the Simpson Effect are mind-boggling. It provides hard evidence for the existence of a group mind, or a collective consciousness. It might well explain the growth of mass movements, whether peaceful or hostile, that can lead to the end of the Cold War or peace in Northern Ireland – or, on the other hand, to the rise to power of a Hitler or a Stalin. We may all have more control over world affairs than we think.

PK ON DEMAND

PK can take place to order under the appropriate conditions. In the 1850s, one of the most popular parlour games involved sitting round a table and talking to it – or rather to the spirits who were thought to be using it to tap out mes-sages in a primitive Morse code (one rap for yes, two for no and so on). This came about as the result of one of the most extra-ordinary episodes in the social history of the 19th century, the sudden rise of spiritualism that followed an unusually well-witnessed poltergeist case in the home of the Fox family of Hydesville, NY.

Spiritualists were thrilled to be able to communicate with their departed loved ones, or so they believed. Yet non-spiritu-alists took to the tables just as eagerly, and some went about their new pastime in a strictly scientific way. One of the first of these researchers was Alfred

"I am not saying all this is possible. I am saying it is true."

Russel Wallace, the joint dis-coverer of what has rather unfairly come to be known as Darwinism, or natural selection.

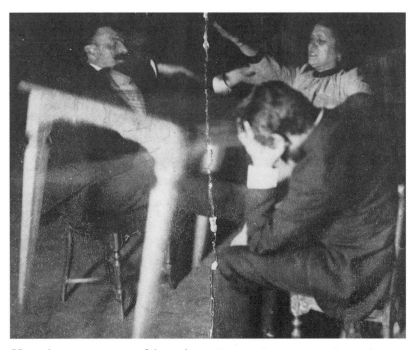

Here is an account of how he described his early experiences in PK: "We stood round a small work-table, placing our hands all close together near the centre. After a short time the table would rock about from side to side, and then, appearing to steady itself, would rise vertically from six inches to a foot, and remain suspended often for 15 or 20 seconds. During this

EUSAPIA PALLADINO: *The medium (top right) raises a table in one of the earliest known photographs of psychokinesis in action (dated 1903, London). Was it genuine, or just another hoax?*

time any two of the party could strike it or press on it, as it resisted a very considerable force." Wallace also said he could hear: "tapping, rapping, thumping, slapping, scratching and rubbing" sounds, which could even beat time when a tune was whistled. These, he said, could hardly be caused by "unconscious muscular activity", an explanation put forward by sceptics at the time.

Another early researcher was a young man who was later to become one of the leading scientists of his day, Sir William Crookes. He carried out a series of experiments in his own laboratory with the man generally recognised as the leading medium of all time, Daniel Dunglas Home. Here are some of the PK phenomena which this highly qualified researcher recorded as early as 1874:

* Percussive and other allied sounds. Movements of heavy substances when at a distance from the medium
* The rising of tables and chairs off the ground, without contact with any person
* The levitation of human beings
* The appearance of hands, either self-luminous or visible by ordinary light
* Luminous appearances
* Direct writing
* Movement of heavy substances when at distance from the medium
* Phantom forum and faces

These observations were compiled, let us remember, by a future president of the Royal Society. Crookes was condemned by his contemporaries, who steadfastly refused to accept even the possibility of PK, to which he retorted: "I am not saying all this is possible. I am saying it is true."

PSI IN ACTION

"QUITE BY CHANCE, I HAD THE OPPORTUNITY TO TEST MATTHEW'S UNIQUE HEALING SKILLS — ON MYSELF..."

We have looked at the evidence for telepathy, clairvoyance, precognition and PK. A couple of questions arise here – can they be put to good (or bad) use? Can they help you get rich? The answer to both questions is yes.

Perhaps the most remarkable "miracle cure" of all was that of an unnamed boy in his teens who suffered from a condition, popularly and misleadingly, known as fish-skin disease. Victims have in fact no proper skin at all, and are covered with an extremely unattractive substance that makes life both totally miserable and usually brief. Several attempts to perform a transplant from a small area of normal skin on the boy's chest failed. So the anaesthetist at the Queen Victoria Hospital in East Grinstead, tried one last treatment. He decided to use some mind power.

From what little he could see of the boy's body, he mistakenly thought it was just a case of multiple warts, and he knew that warts could sometimes be removed by hypnosis. So he put the patient in a hypnotic trance and simply told him to come back the following week with an arm clear of warts. They would just fall off, he said. And so they did. Just a few days later, the hypnotist, Dr Albert Mason, was demonstrating to the Royal Society of Medicine what was probably the first case on record of a successful cure for this kind of disease. Further hypnotic treatment produced further improvement.

IMPOSSIBLE TO CURE?

It was not a complete cure, but a follow-up examination four years later showed that the boy was now leading a normal life, having received no treatment other than that of Dr Mason. Curiously enough, he had attempted several other cases of the same disease without any further success.

How could such an 'impossible' cure have taken place? Dr Mason tried to explain: "I suppose it means that potentially anything can be done, since we have the embryonic possibilities within our skin." However, neither he nor anybody else seems to have faced the implications of this remark. The founding of the Royal College of Hypnosis is long overdue.

Another healer who has demonstrated the power of the mind is Matthew Manning. In 1975 I suffered from a slipped disc, which left me unable to use my right hand for writing. I tried every conventional form of treatment without any success. Then, quite by chance, I had the opportunity to test Matthew's unique healing skills – on myself.

He was making a short film for the American series That's Incredible, for which I had undertaken the research. Three patients had been invited to come and be healed live on camera. When one of them did not turn up, I offered to fill the vacancy. This was about five years after my slipped disc, and the ulnar nerve leading to my fingers had very gradually begun to repair itself, as I had been told it would. But I could still not write or play the piano with my right hand.

Later that day, I could once again do both – and now, 20 years later, I still can.

It was a curious experience. Matthew put a hand on the back of my neck. After a few minutes I felt a sudden burst of heat, as if he was pressing a fairly warm iron against me. After about 20 minutes, he said he had done all he could for the time being, and I could come for a follow-up session if I wanted to. I never had to do this, and immediately after the session, in which I happened to be sitting on a stool at a grand piano, I was delighted to find I could play a scale with all the fingers of my right hand.

NATURAL ENERGY

Scientific tests carried out at the Menninger Foundation in the USA, by Drs Elmer and Alyce Green have shown that certain individual healers really do have powers of some kind. Dr Elmer Green had this to say

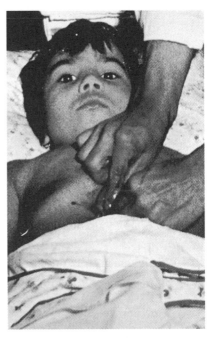

MIND OVER MATTER? *A young patient feels no pain as Brazilian psychic surgeon Edivaldo Oliveira Silva operates on him.*

45

about his tests: "In some of the healers we have studied we found voltage surges of maybe 80 volts. The whole body will change voltage by 80 volts. That's not possible. Except for the fact that it happens."

Many healers are convinced they are channels for divine energy that comes from God. Some believe they are being guided by the spirit of a deceased doctor or a native American. Others see healers as transformers of a natural energy that flows through them and into their patients.

Perhaps the most sensible remark concerning the healing process comes from Major Bruce Macmanaway, a former army officer, who discovered his own abilities while attending to wounded troops in the evacuation of Dunkirk, and went on to become one of Britain's most respected practitioners. "We may not understand the healing energy," he wrote in his autobiography, "but it appears to be available for human use." At this point in time, all we know for certain is that in the right hands it can literally work wonders.

DON'T SPARE THE ROD

In 1952, the Royal Engineers began building a £14 million military base in Germany, with Colonel Harry Grattan in charge. The project was faced with a crisis because the local geologists simply could not find enough water to supply such a large base. So, driven by urgent need, he provided his own solution – with his dowsing rod.

He eventually located a source of water that had never been tapped before, and rescued the whole project.

Dowsing can in fact be used to find almost anything, from precious minerals to missing persons and dead bodies. It is most often used to find water, however, and is used by more farmers, local authorities, governments and multinational companies than the few who are willing to admit it publicly.

One that is glad to go public on the matter is Germany's official overseas aid organisation, the GTZ. Not only has it used this method to find water for the past 15 years; it has also success. In the first of his major projects to be monitored by Professor Betz, a total of 691 drillings were made. Only four per cent of these turned out to be dry. This compares with 70 per cent of drillings in the area being dry when companies used conventional methods to find water. Betz was extremely impressed, and he labelled Schröter a 'super-hydrologist'.

Divining is used by farmers, governments and multinational companies...

welcomed the serious scientific investigation of dowsing conducted by the team led by Professor Hans-Dieter Betz of the University of Munich.

Research on a large scale began in 1981, with 500 dowsers being tested. The best of these, an aid worker named Hans Schröter, has been finding water all over the world ever since, often with spectacular Again and again he has succeeded where years and years of orthodox geological wisdom has failed. A typical case involved a township in the Kalahari Desert, where 17 wells had been drilled. Only one was productive, meaning that the region's water supply was not safe. On his very first day on the job, Schröter indicated two sites he considered promising.

47

The first one produced a water source good enough to provide the whole township with all the water it needed.

Scientists in Britain are now also taking an interest in dowsing. Professor Vincent Reddish of Edinburgh University carried out a series of tests in the early nineties which satisfied him that: "We are dealing with a real physical force, as real as gravity and magnetism, not some mysterious psychical effect." Cambridge engineer Dr Anne Miller is equally uncompromising: "There is incontrovertible evidence that dowsing works," she concluded in a 1998 lecture.

One person who has made very profitable use of it is Uri Geller. He embarked on his career as a dowser chiefly of oil and minerals on the advice of Sir Val Duncan, chairman of Rio Tinto-Zinc, one of Britain's largest mining companies.

REAL MONEY

Sir Val was a dowser himself, and it was he who taught Uri how to do it. He also told him this was a way to make 'real money' – hence my earlier reference to a 'psi millionaire'.

Opinions as to how dowsing works differ as widely as they do on the question of healing, and there are those who are not so sure that 'mysterious psychical effects' can be ruled out. If dowsing involves the use of a 'real physical force', it should be possible to measure such a force. Yet it is not, any more than it is possible to measure whatever the remote viewers described in Chapter 2 are doing. For the time being then, we must be content with the knowledge that however it works, dowsing, like healing, is 'available for human use'.

HAPPY MEDIUM

"I SAW HIM SLOWLY RISE UP WITH A CONTINUOUS
GLIDING MOVEMENT AND REMAIN ABOUT
SIX INCHES OFF THE GROUND..."

The above quote is not the statement of some deluded occultist, but a Fellow of the Royal Society – and its eventual president, Sir William Crookes. He was one of the most brilliant minds of his generation, inventor of the vacuum tube and the radiometer, and his scientific observations should not be lightly ignored.

There were more extraordinary observations included in his detailed study of the powers of medium Daniel Home. For example: "We had scarcely sat down a minute when raps were heard from different parts of the table: a strong vibration of our chairs and the table was felt, and sounds like thumps on the floor were heard. A curious metallic tapping sound was also heard on the iron screw of the table."

On Home's most controversial abilities, he remarked: "The best cases of Home's levitation I witnessed were in my own house. On one occasion he went to a clear part of the room and, after standing quietly for a minute, told us he was rising. I saw him slowly rise up with a continuous gliding movement and remain about six inches off the ground for several seconds ... On another occasion, I was invited to come to him when he rose 18 inches, and passed my hands under his feet, round him, and over his head when he was in the air."

Daniel Dunglas Home was what we call a medium. Just as 'the media' collect bits of information and pictures and convey them to us in newspapers and on radio or television, a human medium conveys information or action from an unknown source. Many believe (as Home did) that this source is the spirit world, which we will be exploring in a later chapter.

PHYSICAL ACTIVITY WE CANNOT EXPLAIN

Human mediums can be either mental or physical, or indeed both. The former convey information and the latter produce physical activity of a kind that we cannot explain in terms of present scientific knowledge. This is why there are those who prefer to ignore them altogether, or to assume that all mediums are frauds, which they are not. This attitude has led to a postponement of investigation into something that would surely have considerable practical value to mankind.

EARLIEST ATTEMPTS TO RECORD PK

Telekinesis, a word no longer in general use by psi researchers, implies PK at long distance. It was also observed and carefully measured in a classic series of experiments held in Paris in 1930, with a modest young Austrian car mechanic named Rudi Schneider, acting as the medium. One of his investigators, Dr Eugène Osty, rigged up an ingenious apparatus with which he was able to establish that Rudi had been able to influence an infra-red beam at a distance. This was one of the earliest successful attempts to provide scientifically recorded evidence for PK.

Schneider was also one of the first PK mediums to allow himself to be rigorously examined in action by an eminent magician. On a visit to London in 1929 the founder and president of the Magicians' Club, Will Goldston, went over every inch of the séance room without finding anything suspicious, and still reported:

"We saw the stool on which stood the basket illuminated by phosphorous paint move towards us. It moved in a peculiar way and then suddenly toppled over. Curtains flew apart. We felt a fearful icy draft blowing. It was uncanny. I watched keenly for signs of trickery but saw none ... No group of my fellow magicians could have produced those effects under those conditions."

A BIRD ON THE SHOULDER

The name Teofil Modrzejewski is hardly known to the general public today, and was entirely unknown during his lifetime up to his death in 1943, except as that of a Polish poet and journalist, who worked in a bank.

Yet he led a Jekyll and Hyde existence and, under the better known pseudonym of Franek Kluski, he became one of the most thoroughly studied PK mediums of all time. Some of the phenomena witnessed in his presence were among the strangest on record. He would often create 'spirit gloves' – wax moulds of hands supposedly produced by the dead.

A large number of investigators, including the French Nobel laureate, Charles Richet, testified to the reality of his abilities, and a large quantity of photographs were taken during his séances. If it were not for this evidence, one might well be tempted to conclude that Kluski was just an extremely accomplished magician.

Richet listed his findings: "Light phenomena, starting with merely points of light all the way to fairly strong lights of various shapes and colours; touching by materialised body members, rustling, sounds of steps, murmurs; sliding, levitat-

It is worth remembering that Kluski not only insisted on his real name never being used in connection with his medium- istic activity, he also never received any payment and, despite some intense scrutiny, he was never caught faking.

His séances were attended by a total of about 350 people, none of whom ever attempted to unmask him. Although it is

"As we watched we saw the ectoplasm begin to emerge slowly from the medium's mouth..."

ion ... materialisations of hands, faces, heads and complete human figures, which illumi- nated themselves with their own light or with the aid of a phosphorescent screen."

One photograph shows what appears to be an ectoplasmic cord emerging from his hand. Another clearly shows a large bird perched on his shoulder.

tempting to think he simply took advantage of a more gullible age, he continues to baffle researchers today just as he did 80 years ago.

"O that this too too solid flesh would melt," said Hamlet, and there is abundant evidence from the séance room that this is just what it can do on occa- sions. It does not dissolve into a dew, as Hamlet hoped, but into that legendary substance known as ectoplasm, eventually vanishing altogether.

ECTOPLASM

The word was coined by Richet, and ectoplasm has been defined as "a mysterious proto-plasmic substance streaming out of the body of mediums" which condenses into the form of solid and apparently living people. It is such a bizarre phe-nomenon that it would not be mentioned here if it were not for the vast amount of evidence of its existence.

Its presence, and its extraor-dinary qualities have reportedly been witnessed by hundreds of researchers. It has been pho-tographed and even filmed briefly, and samples of it have been analysed and described as 'albuminoid matter accompa-nied by fatty matter and cells found in the human organism'.

PHYSICAL MATERIALISATIONS

Here is a typical account of the way ectoplasm appears, in this case from the Welsh medium Alec Harris: "As we watched we saw the ectoplasm begin to emerge slowly from the medium's mouth, nose and ears, it rolled down his body on to the floor where it coiled itself into a sizeable mass, and from the centre of this mass it began to rise, just as if someone were pushing it upwards."

This mass then took the form of a perfect and easily recognisable human being, which then duly dissolved and became re-absorbed in the medium's body. On several other occasions, so I have been informed by two eye-witnesses – attending separate séances, but reporting similar effects – the materialised form would gradually shrink and seem to disappear into the floor.

Reports of materialisations of human forms date back to the early 1850s, two of the earliest mediums being Leah and Kate Fox, members of the family whose experiences in their home at Hydesville, New York, led to the birth of spiritualism.

INTO THE ARK

With the death of Alec Harris in 1974, the age of PK and mediums who could produce actual physical materialisations seemed to have come to an end. But it did survive, in fact, in the form of private home séances across the country. Most of these prefer to adopt a low profile and keep the media (and researchers) at bay.

Luckily, the situation has improved in recent years with the founding of the Noah's Ark Society by Robin Foy in 1990. Its stated aim was "to promote and develop physical mediumship", and it has made great progress in its early years, holding regular seminars, at which participants are usually able to attend a séance with an experienced medium or group.

One of the earliest Noah's Ark Society members was a young man named Colin Fry, who had no previous experience of mediumship. Yet within a year, he had been able to produce an impressive range of phenomena. One of his specialities, is to be securely tied to a chair using telephone clips, which cannot be undone and have to be cut open, and then discovered after the dark séance with the clips still in place – but without his coat on.

We will, I am sure, be hearing more of him. A new age of physical mediumship has begun, and with all the wonders of modern technology, it should soon be possible to finally come up with the evidence to satisfy all doubters.

WHO WROTE THAT?

...ALTHOUGH THE POEMS WERE INDEED IN HIS OWN HANDWRITING, THE REAL AUTHORS WERE THE DECEASED POETS THEMSELVES...

Critics were amazed when an astonishing 421-page volume of poetry, containing 259 poems signed by 56 poets , was first published in Rio de Janeiro, Brazil in 1932. It became an instant bestseller, and it is still in print today. The poets represented included just about every single major name in Brazilian and Portuguese literature, and it was agreed that the poems were of high quality. There were, however, several unusual features of this volume. The first was its title – Parnassus From Beyond the Grave. The second was that every one of the poems came from the hand of the same man, 22-year-old Francisco Candido Xavier. He insisted that although the poems were undeniably in his own handwriting, the real authors were the deceased poets themselves.

'Chico Xavier', as everybody in Brazil knows him, began his literary career in a wholly unexpected way. One day at school he won an honourable mention for an essay on Brazil for a competition held by the state government. He then caused a stir by telling his teacher that it had been dictated to him by a spirit. He was asked if he could prove this claim by writing an essay on the blackboard, on a subject to be suggested by one of his fellow pupils.

One of them suggested 'Sand'. When the laughter had subsided, Chico went to the board and began writing at once: "My sons, creation is not mocked. A grain of sand is known celebrities in Brazil, thanks to the steady stream of poems, novels and works of non-fiction that followed the publication of Parnassus.

HARD EVIDENCE

What Chico does (he is still alive and working, though now in his late eighties) is known as automatic writing. This is a particularly convincing form of

"...A grain of sand is almost nothing, yet it appears as a tiny star reflecting the sun of God..."

almost nothing, yet it appears as a tiny star reflecting the sun of God..." Chico, it was clear, was a medium.

He left school at 13, working in a shop and a factory before getting a very modest job with the Ministry of Agriculture, where he remained until he retired in 1961. By then, Chico had become one of the best- mental mediumship because it produces hard evidence that would be very hard to fake. One of Chico's longest works, a 553-page novel set in first-century Rome, took him just eight months to complete. Lew Wallace's Ben Hur, by comparison, took eight years. Moreover, Chico's custom is to do all his writing in public, at weekly sessions at his local spiritist centre in the interior town of Uberaba. He sits at a table, puts his left hand over his eyes and turns his head to one side while his right hand covers page after page at tremendous speed and without hesitation. An assistant has to pull away the finished pages so as not to interrupt the flow.

Total sales of Chico's book have run into the millions, yet he has never asked for, nor received, a penny for any of them. All the proceeds have been given to charity through various spiritist organisations.

SUBCONSCIOUS

The usual explanation for automatic writing is that it originates from the subconscious mind. Yet the question arises: if Chico's huge output – much of it, Brazilian colleagues have assured me, of very high literary quality – came from his subconscious, how did it get there in the first place? Is there any plausible alternative to Chico's own opinion: that it was dictated to him by discarnate entities, or spirits? Who are we to disagree with the poet Augusto do Anjos, who purportedly dictated a sonnet called 'Ego Sum' (I Am) to Chico while he was on a visit to the poet's birthplace? It contained the following lines:

"Eu sou quem eu sou.
Extremamente injusto
Seria, então, se não vos
declarasse
Se vos mentisse, se
mistificasse
No anonimato, sendo
eu o Augusto."

(I am who I am. It would be extremely unjust, therefore, if I did not declare myself, if I lied or deceived you in anonymity, since I am Augusto.)

THE AUTOMATIC ARTIST

LUIZ GASPARETTO:

The Brazilian trance artist produces a drawing, signed 'Renoir', in just 35 seconds.

Luiz Gasparetto is a Brazilian clinical psychologist who is also a spiritist medium. His speciality is automatic 'art'; watching him at work is quite an experience. He sits quietly at a table in a room lit by weak red light with a pile of paper and a box of crayons in front of him. He puts a hand over his eyes and turns his head, just as his compatriot Chico Xavier does, as if deliberately trying not to see what he is doing. Somebody switches on a cassette of Vivaldi's The Four Seasons, and Luiz is off.

He grabs a crayon and draws the outline of a face, attacking the paper so hard that it starts to slide around on the pile.

The portrait is finished and signed 'Renoir'. It has taken just 35 seconds

Art can be produced automatically as well, and I have witnessed some astonishing examples of it being created.

I lean over and put my fingers on its top corners to keep it still. A few more hasty slashes with the crayon and the portrait is finished and signed 'Renoir'. The whole process has taken Luiz, or Renoir, just 35 seconds.

He goes on to produce 13 more drawings in just over an hour. Some are drawn upside down. Some are double portraits drawn with both hands at once. Some are dashed off in a matter of seconds, others are worked on for up to five minutes, several colours being used to sketch in a background or add detail to a dress.

One of the most intriguing features is the way Luiz puts the dots in his invisible sitter's eyes while his own eyes are still closed. Another is the way he can sign two pictures at once with different names. Just try writing 'Manet' with your left hand and 'Modigliani' with your right. I can't do it. As several sceptical experts have testified on television shows in which Luiz has taken part, his works are not likely to be accepted as 'originals' by those he claims sign them. Yet this is not the point. The point is that what Luiz does, cannot be considered normal. Could a trained artist produce a string of pleasing portraits, landscapes and still lifes without even looking at them? I think not.

THROUGH THE GISMO

To many people, the word medium means somebody who conveys messages from the dead. As we shall see later, some have provided good evidence that they can do exactly this, and in the early days of spiritualism some went even better and took photographs of the dead. In the 1860s, William Mumler, a Boston engraver, set up shop as a 'spirit photographer', whose clients were delighted to find their late loved ones hovering in the misty background. Although he ended up in court on a charge

SPIRIT PHOTOGRAPHS: *Boston photographer William Mumler claimed that his pictures (above) recorded the visits of his clients' departed loved ones. He was never caught using any kind of trickery.*

AN UNINVITED GUEST: *(Opposite page) Two photos taken seconds apart. One with flash (top), the other without (below). But who's the woman in the centre of the lower photo? Her skirt can even be seen under the table. Extensive analysis has failed to produce any scientific explanation.*

of fraud, he was acquitted and was never detected in any act of trickery. This could mean that either he was cleverer than his investigators, or that he really did take pictures of spirits.

This may be too much for some readers to take on board, but the Society for Psychical Research has a large collection of photographs in which people can be seen who were not there when the picture was taken.

The witnesses have been thoroughly questioned. They all maintain that they have no idea who the mystery woman is, and insist she was not visible at the time (or before, or since). These things do happen.

There is at least one psi-photographer who cannot be dismissed as a fraud. This is a former bellhop from Chicago, named Ted Serios. What he did was to hold an ordinary card-

They all maintain they have no idea who the mystery woman in the photograph is

I have helped investigate one of these – a photo taken of a group of holidaymakers with an unknown guest in their midst. The negative has since been exhaustively examined by experts who have all confirmed that the image of the woman has not been, and could not possibly have been, superimposed on the original picture.

board or plastic tube about half an inch in diameter – which he called his 'gismo' – in front of a Polaroid camera and produce prints unlike anything seen before. Instead of showing his blurred face, as they should, they showed a bewildering variety of mostly unidentified buildings and streets – anything from an aircraft hangar or a London bus to – most intriguingly – a Soviet spacecraft of which there were no published photos at the time.

Serios was examined by in excess of 30 scientifically trained observers, producing several hundred inexplicable prints. Some of these were all black and some all white. Others had a strange kind of fog swirling around. In one instance, images even turned up when Serios was more than 20 yards away.

His various gismos were examined and found not to contain anything at all suspicious. Cynics were sure they were going to find bits of transparencies, as used by magicians. But try as they might, they did not. When he left the scene in the 1970s, reportedly to pursue his true vocation of getting drunk, his reputation was still intact. His mysterious ability remains unexplained to this day.

EXTRUSIONS

Strange photographs of a quite different kind were produced by the healer Olga Worrall when she paid a visit to the Los Angeles laboratory of psi researcher Dr Thelma Moss. After doing some experiments which appeared to show that she could affect the energy field of enzymes, she suggested one of her own. Going into the darkroom, she picked up a sheet of film and then simply held it between her fingertips for a few minutes.

When the film was dropped into the developing dish, they watched as what Dr Moss described as a 'textured cheese-cloth' pattern appeared, unlike anything she had seen before. It was not really even like cheesecloth, which is woven in fine straight lines. This pattern was irregular, but with a few straight lines here and there and also several curves and gaps, as if somebody's knitting had gone badly wrong. Some of the threads seemed to disappear altogether. Could this be some kind of ectoplasm? Olga Worrall agreed it could be and probably was. What else could it be?

Dr Moss kindly sent me a copy of the photograph. When I passed it on to a scientist I knew at Imperial College, asking for an expert analysis, he was firmly convinced it showed a physical presence.

"We think it's just some kind of extruded plastic," he said. At no point had I told him anything about how this peculiar image was taken. His reply seemed to confirm the astonishing truth about what could be one of the most significant photographs ever taken – and without a camera at that – the first true picture of ectoplasm.

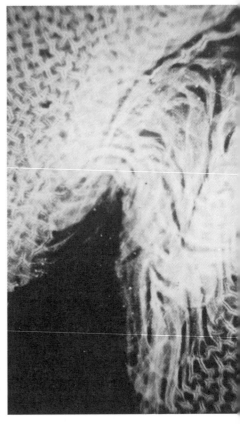

ECTOPLASM? *Olga Worrall created this image simply by touching photographic film.*

I HAVE DIED

HE THEN HAD THE FEELING
OF BEING ENVELOPED IN LIGHT,
WARMTH AND LOVE.

Can there really be life after death? The obvious, logical answer is no, because death means the termination of life. So let us put the question in a different way: is death the end of conscious existence? To find out the answer to this question, why not ask those who have died and, as you might say, lived to tell the amazing tale?

In 1986, David Verdegaal, a Lincolnshire businessman, had a massive heart attack in an Austrian hotel. On the journey to hospital, his heart stopped beating. However, this was by no means the end of him. As he recalled in an interview he gave a few years later, "The first thing I was conscious of was the fact that I had died."

He then had a feeling of being enveloped in love, light and warmth "as though I was a little child being cuddled by God". He next found himself at a kind of heavenly checkpoint – in his case, a gate at the end of a garden. He went through, but immediately felt he should go back.

And go back he did, to the Innsbruck hospital where the cardiac team managed to restart his heart at their fourth try. They reckoned it had been stopped for half an hour – longer than the period from which a recovery can be made.

Mr Verdegaal remained in a coma while being flown back to England in an air ambulance. The head of the hospital's cardiac care department later said, "I left him without any hope that he would recover."

The patient, however, had already recovered to the extent of being aware of what was going on. He saw a stretcher being wheeled into the air ambulance. "I was watching from above, not really taking in that it was me." He soon realised that it was him, though, and that "if I could make it through this one night, I would make it all the way back". He did make it all the way back, and eight years later was so confident of his recovery, he actually ran two marathons.

In 1994, the Dutch cardiologist Doctor Pim van Lommel revealed the fascinating results of a survey of all patients at ten hospitals who had undergone 'clinical death' over the previous four years. There were 345 of them, and no less than 62 reported having had some kind of what is known as an NDE, or Near Death Experience. Here are their typical experiences:

* a feeling of calm
* the sensation of leaving the body
* going down a tunnel towards a bright light
* meeting dead relatives
* deciding or being ordered to 'go back'

THE TENNIS SHOE MYSTERY

One of the most famous of all NDEs was that of a woman known only as Maria, whose heart stopped beating in a Seattle hospital noted for its high standard of coronary care. The emergency team got her heart going again with some difficulty, but a few hours later it looked as though Maria was going to have another attack. She seemed very agitated about something, so a social worker named Kimberley Clark Sharp went to calm her down and ask what was the matter?

"I saw it," Maria explained. "I saw it all." She went on to give an exact description of the resuscitation techniques that had been used on her, even

level, but had floated outside the building altogether and noticed a tennis shoe on a window ledge. She described it in detail – it was blue, worn on one side and its laces were under the heel. She begged the social worker to go and fetch it.

Kimberley Sharp did find the shoe. Unlike most tennis shoes, it was indeed blue, and it was worn on one side and placed with the lace under the heel, exactly as Maria had described. The incident made such an impression on the social worker

She had not only been floating around the room at ceiling level, but had floated outside the building altogether...

noting such details as the paper from a machine (the electro-cardiograph) spilling onto the floor and a man punching her chest. And there was more – she had not only been floating around the room at ceiling

that she went on to become leader of the local branch of the International Association for Near Death Studies (IANDS).

Incidents such as these do not prove life after death, but they make it seem a good deal more possible. If part of our consciousness can leave the body altogether, then it is clear that our soul does not need the physical body at all. Why, therefore, should the death of a physical body affect it? As J B Priestley put it: "Consciousness can survive the death of body and brain because while they inform it and strongly influence it, they don't own it."

RECURRENT NIGHTMARES

Striking evidence has begun to come in over the last few years, indicating that recipients of organ transplants can sometimes get more than a new organ. They also acquire something of the personality of the deceased donor, occasionally even clear memories. Dr Paul Pearsall reports one extraordinary case in which an eight-year-old girl, who had received the heart of a slightly older girl who had been murdered, began

to have recurrent nightmares in which she clearly saw the man who had killed her donor. Her concerned mother eventually felt obliged to notify the police. The little girl was asked to give a detailed description of the man in her dreams, and incredibly, within a few weeks a man was caught and convicted.

What cases like this prove is still uncertain, but it does seem possible that part of our consciousness can survive the death of the brain. Those who advocate transplanting animal organs into human bodies must think long and hard about the possible implications.

MEMORIES OF FORMER INCARNATIONS

"Souls," said Plato "are continuously born over again into this life," and they could hardly do that if they did not survive their previous lives. There is now a vast amount of evidence that suggests Plato was right.

This is mainly thanks to all the efforts of Professor Ian Stevenson, who was head of the Department of Psychiatry at the University of Virginia, and whose first publication on 'claimed memories of former incarnations', dates from 1960. A few years later, he wrote a book summarising twenty cases which he found "suggestive of reincarnation". And ever since then he has been travelling the world and amassing a huge collection of such cases.

Some of these are indeed suggestive, such as that of Cemil Fahrici, who was born in 1935 in a town near the Turkish–Syrian border. The name his parents gave him was not Cemil but Dahham, though almost as soon as he could talk, the boy began to insist on being addressed as Cemil. He also started to have nightmares about being involved in a gun-fight with police. There was something else unusual about him – a birthmark on his neck which had to be stitched soon after he was born, leaving behind a permanent scar.

As it happened, just three days before Dahham/Cemil was born, a notorious gangster named Cemil Hayik had died in a siege, shooting himself in the head. The young Cemil seemed to know all about this, and clearly knew a lot more about his dead namesake than he should have.

It was the birthmark, however, that made the case in question unusually persuasive. When Professor Stevenson met the adult Cemil Fahrici, he was fascinated to discover a second birthmark, on top of his head – in exactly the spot one would expect it to be if Hayik had placed his gun under his chin and aimed upwards.

Belief in reincarnation is extensive among people of widely differing religious groups, most notably the Buddhists and the Hindus of Southeast Asia.

Stevenson reckons that this belief is most likely to have started in ancient times when people had direct experience of it, probably in the form of memories of past lives. And, as several recent widely publicised cases show, people are still having such experiences.

One of the best known British cases of recent times is that of the Pollock twins, Gillian and Jennifer. They were born in Hexham in 1958, the second set of twins in the family. The others, Joanna and Jacqueline, had been run over and killed the previous year. Their father, a devout Roman Catholic who did not share his church's views on reincarnation, had actually prayed to God, asking for his dead twin daughters to be returned to him.

So they were – or at least so it seemed to their parents. Jennifer had a birthmark identical to Jacqueline's. She also had a thin line on her forehead, just

Their father had prayed to God asking for his dead daughters to be returned...

like the one Jacqueline had after falling off her tricycle.

The Pollocks moved from Hexham to Whitley Bay four months after the new twins' birth, and when the girls were three, they visited Hexham for the first time. Here, they immediately and inexplicably identified their old house and school, despite never having seen photographs of either.

They would frequently talk about the accident which killed

their older twin sisters, and despite being told not to by their parents, they even played games based on it. One day, Florence Pollock found Gillian holding Jennifer's head and saying something about "blood coming from her eyes, because that's where the car hit her".

HIS MOTHER HAD COME BACK TO EARTH

Their memories faded, as is often the case, though this did not apply to Jenny Cockell. She was in her late thirties when she wrote Yesterday's Children, her best-selling account of her previous life and death in Ireland. Her memories had begun when she was a child, with vivid dreams of a house in a place she was later to identify as Malahide, near Dublin. She not only discovered who she had been in her previous life, but managed to track down four of her sons, at least one of

whom fully accepted that his mother had come back to earth. A controversial feature of Jenny Cockell's case is the fact that part of her past-life recall came while she was under hypnosis. This is a notoriously unreliable way to obtain accurate information, whether about this life or any other, and some (though not all) of the details she produced while in trance turned out to be wrong.

DÉJÀ VU

The feeling that we have been somewhere before is most commonly experienced in flashes of 'déjà vu' – French for 'already seen'. In Pictures from Italy Charles Dickens described an experience of this kind. On a walking tour he came across "a little scene, which seemed perfectly familiar to me" and noted that "if I had been murdered there in some former life I could not have remembered the place more thoroughly". Recently, the artist Hortense Kelly painted an imaginary picture of a village in Spain. She then went on holiday to Spain and was startled to find an exactly identical village.

Cases such as these could, of course, be instances of memories from a previous life. The problem is, that it is next to impossible to prove that those who have déjà vu experiences have never seen the places in question before – on a postcard or in a film – and have retained the memory without being consciously aware of it.

NEW SOULS

Although a strong case can be made for reincarnation, there is one drawback. It has been pointed out that we can't all have been here before. Simple mathematics demonstrates that because of the global population explosion, there are more of us alive today than there ever have been throughout the entire history of the planet.

However, we have no way of disproving the possibility that 'new souls' can come into being and that many of us are on our first time round.

Professor Stevenson does not claim to have proved the existence of reincarnation. But he does believe he has helped bring the belief out of the realm of superstition. He comments: "The evidence is far from conclusive, but it is now sufficiently strong so that rational persons can believe in it on the basis of evidence, instead of resting their belief on religious traditions only."

ALAS, POOR GHOST

"I LEFT THE HOUSE LIKE A ROCKET. I WAS SCARED. I CAME BACK AND SAID TO MY WIFE, 'IN NO WAY DO I GO BACK INTO THAT HOUSE ON MY OWN.'"

Since there is a great deal of evidence to suggest that we can survive physical death to be born again – the question arises how do we pass the time between dying and coming back to life? Curiously enough, although memories of earlier lives can be quite clear and detailed, recollection of the in-between lives period are distinctly hazy. The best evidence for this state comes not from those who are in it, but from those who come into contact with them. There is absolutely no doubt that people do see ghosts. One was seen one night by a prisoner in an American jail. He said, that as he lay on his bed, "I suddenly, with a start, became aware of a man sitting beside me in my chair." The man looked well dressed, and had "an Asian cast of countenance". The prisoner went on to say he saw the ghost "as plainly as I see anyone I look at. Then, suddenly as he had come, he was gone." The prisoner in question was one Malcolm X, a prominent black rights activist, who had nothing to gain – and quite a bit to lose – by making up stories like this one.

Here is another example, from my own taped interview with the witness:

"I turned to my right, looking directly towards the kitchen. And there I saw, sitting at the living-room table, a man." The witness gave me a detailed description of the man's appearance and dress, insisting, as Malcolm X did, that he looked just as real as anybody

It was indeed. The witness was John Burcombe, uncle of the children that were involved in the Enfield poltergeist case of 1977–78, which my colleague Maurice Grosse and I spent more than a year investigating.

We came to know and trust Mr Burcombe completely, and there is no doubt – he saw a ghost. We discovered that the phantom fitted the description

Like a perfectly normal person sitting at a table. No haziness, no nothing…

else. "Like a perfectly normal person sitting at a table. No haziness, no nothing. Clear as a bell." Like Malcolm X's phantom, he just sat there and then was suddenly gone.

"I left the house like a rocket. I was scared. I came back and said to my wife 'Sorry, in no way do I go back into that house on my own. The place is … haunted.'"

of his neighbour's grandfather, long deceased – although there was no way we could prove beyond doubt it was him.

QUEEN'S HOUSE: *A retired Canadian clergyman, Reverend. R W Hardy, took this photo of the Tulip Staircase in the Queen's House, Greenwich. His wife later testified that no person was on the stairs at the time.*

Ghosts are usually believed to be dead, but in fact many apparitions are of those who are still alive or just about to die. Indeed, distant sightings of those on the point of death are so common that only a really desperate sceptic can ignore them. In 1886, three of the founders of the Society for Psychical Research carried out the face of my friend, Miss Grant. I started up in bed and, looking round, saw her figure leaving the room." The housekeeper got up and searched the house, noting that it was just after nine o'clock. She went back to bed feeling uneasy, and certain that something had happened to her friend. The following day a message came,

The most haunted places I have ever been in were a council house and a couple of pubs.

a survey which produced over 700 cases which they believed defied normal explanation.

Here is a typical one: Mrs Duthie, an Edinburgh clergyman's housekeeper, was just settling down for the night, lying half-asleep with her face to the wall, when: "I felt that someone was bending over me, looking into my face. I opened my eyes, and looked up into

telling her that Miss Grant had passed away in Aberdeen at nine o' clock the previous night.

HIGH SPIRITS

When Noel Coward told us that the stately homes of England "provide a lot of chances for psychical research", he was speaking from personal experience. Playing the piano one day at West Wycombe Park, home of the Dashwood family of Hell Fire Club fame, he looked up to see "an amiable, smiling monk, who then disappeared".

It is not only stately homes that are haunted. So are banks, hospitals, theatres and almost every other kind of building. The most haunted places I have ever been in were a council house and a couple of pubs.

The former was the scene of John Burcombe's encounter – mentioned previously – and featured extensive poltergeist activity. The first pub was the picturesque Seven Stars Inn in Robertsbridge, where I was taken by a BBC radio reporter to record a piece for the Colour Supplement programme (Radio 4, 13 October 1985).

We were on our own in a room on the second floor, and I was describing to him the typical kind of activity that can usually be expected in a haunted pub: "pools of water,

outbreaks of fire, maybe plates flying around. That comes later. You always start with either loud knocks or…"

WHUMP! I was about to add "or stones falling from the ceiling" when there was a massive thump coming from the floor just behind the reporter. As the directional microphone was pointing at me, it sounded a good deal louder to us than it did to listeners. It was as if somebody wearing heavy boots had stamped a foot as hard as possible. I had to admire the sense of timing.

If I had been able to complete my list, I would have added apparitions – often seen by more than one witness on different occasions, such as the Seven Stars' resident monk.

I would also have included the following unexplained phenomena: the sound of footsteps on stairs or walking across empty upstairs rooms, outbreaks of PK

BRITAIN'S MOST HAUNTED PUB? *Psi investigator Maurice Gross outside The Kings' Cellars, Croydon.*

(a whole shelf of crockery shot across the kitchen one day at the Seven Stars), cold breezes drifting around, doors opening and closing on their own, pictures falling from secure hooks, beer taps and pumps turning themselves on, as if some thirsty ghost was dying (if that's the right word) for a drink, and cats or dogs suddenly reacting to an invisible presence.

Probably the most haunted pub of all was The Kings' Cellars in Croydon. The full story of this extraordinary case will never be told, several key witnesses being either not available or refusing to talk. It all seems to have begun in the early 1970s, when the pub was only a few years old. A young woman working in the office block next door fell to her death from an 18th floor window, landing on the pub's roof.

Some time later, a young woman was seen sitting in the cellar bar by a member of staff who was about to go up to her and tell her it was before opening time when the intruder "got up and disintegrated".

The same employee saw the same apparition a week later, leaning on the bar after closing time. She was seen yet again in 1979, and also heard by two kitchen staff who reported a moaning noise and the words

"Help me." Then she was seen standing at the food counter, and described in detail.

"How did you know it was a ghost?" I asked the witness less than a week after the sighting. "It was the sort of bluish haze-like aura around her," she replied. Plus, of course, the fact that the ghost had dematerialised in front of her eyes.

Then began the main event. Kitchen plates and candles took off from the tables, some landing without breaking, others not. A mysterious fireball made its way up a wall and half way across the ceiling. Glasses shot off their rack so often that the barman stopped hanging them up. On one occasion, 15 of them were found smashed in the middle of the floor when the bar was closed. A beer glass filled itself exactly to the brim. Electronic tills went haywire even after being checked by the supplier.

ONE MANAGER DROPPED DEAD ON THE STAIRS

All of this began to affect the staff and, over the years, at least a dozen managers came and went. One dropped dead on the stairs leading down to the cellar bar. Several marriages came apart, one wife simply walking out one day after seeing something she refused to talk about. It came to the point where Whitbreads, the owners, installed their chief troubleshooter as temporary manager. He too not only left the Kings' Cellars, but he left the country and was last heard of living somewhere in Africa.

The place was then closed down, completely refitted and renamed Goody's Wine Bar. It has since been renamed The Kings' Cellars, and on a recent visit I was very relieved to hear that all had been quiet for the last few years. It now looks just like a perfectly normal pub.

This was a case of poltergeist activity. There is much argument among researchers over whether a poltergeist is a ghost at all. The word is misleading, because it is not a thing, but a way in which things behave.

LOW SPIRITS

The poltergeist can behave extremely badly indeed. Many people are unaware that William Peter Blatty's novel The Exorcist, and the film of the same name, were based (very loosely) on a real case. It took place between January and kept a detailed diary of events, the case began as a typical poltergeist one, with many of the usual symptoms – including knocking, scratching noises, bed-shaking, chairs falling over and the boy being dragged along the floor.

His parents turned to their Lutheran pastor for help, and it was he who recommended that they should seek advice from a Catholic priest. Over the following months at least nine priests, witnessed repeated and prolonged outbursts of violent behaviour in which one had

Many people are unaware that the novel The Exorcist was based on a real case...

May 1949 somewhere in the Washington D C area – nobody is quite sure exactly where – and the victim was in fact not a girl, but a 14-year-old boy. By all accounts, including that of Father Raymond Bishop who his nose broken, and another needed a hundred stitches after being savagely slashed on the arm with a bed spring.

The boy was forcibly baptised a Catholic, whereupon he tried to strangle his mother and, according to Father Bishop, "the usual spitting, gyrating, cursing and physical violence continued until 11.30pm". The following day was simply described as one of "fifteen hours of rage". At the boy's first communion, he ripped pages priests after which she died, apparently from starvation. The priests were found guilty of negligent manslaughter and given suspended sentences. This was a particularly tragic case of what we might call 'deliverance into evil', in which

"The usual spitting, gyrating, cursing and physical violence continued..."

out of the Rituale Romanum and tried to throttle the priest for good measure.

The case did eventually end as suddenly as it had begun, the way these things do whether there are any exorcists involved or not. The question remains whether the exorcists solved the problem or prolonged and intensified it. Several subsequent cases suggest the latter.

In 1976, Anneliese Michel, a German theology student, underwent no less than 67 exorcisms from two Catholic there was no sign of traditional poltergeist activity but clear signs of a disturbed brain in need of urgent medical help.

Exorcism can succeed – it seems to be more a question of who does it, rather than what is done. Two well-known practitioners were the late Canon John Pearce-Higgins, a former vice-provost of Southwark Cathedral, and the Reverend Christopher Neil-Smith, a North London parish priest. In a discussion with Pearce-Higgins on poltergeists and possession, he surprised me by saying, "In the majority of cases you are only dealing with a distressed human being at one remove." He did this by using what he preferred to call intercession – entreaty and prayer on behalf of both victim and disturbing entity – which he used successfully on a case I investigated in South London.

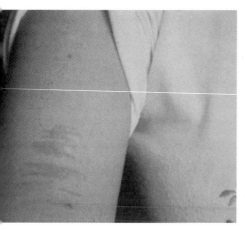

ROTHERHITHE POLTERGEIST CASE: *These scratches were photo-graphed by the author as they were spontaneously appearing on the arm of this victim of a South London poltergeist.*

In this instance, a young woman suffered a poltergeist attack that included a very rare symptom – scratches appearing on her arms, legs and chest. Together with a colleague, I was able to see these scratches suddenly appear and bleed – with no apparent cause. I was also able to photograph them.

Exorcism, as Reverend Neil-Smith practised it, was dramatic stuff. He would stand in front of his altar, grab the patient firmly by the hands and then stretch them out in the form of a cross, then literally force out the invading entity.

Why were he and Canon Pearce-Higgins so successful where many other exorcists had failed? Perhaps because instead of clinging to the belief that poltergeists are agents of the devil, they treated them as what they actually appear to be – independent entities of some kind, crying out for help.

THE TRUTH

As I promised earlier, the truth is in here, and here it is. One of the following statements must definitely be true:

1 Everything described in this book is total fabrication.

2 Things are not what scientists tell us they are.

If the first statement is accepted as true, then here are just a few other things that also have to be true:

★ Upton Sinclair wasted a year of his life either deceiving or being deceived by his wife, then writing a book on telepathy which would certainly have done his reputation as a social reformer more harm than good.

★ All those correct precognitive dreams at the Maimonides laboratory were just lucky guesses – which Malcolm Bessent made repeatedly, under controlled conditions.

★ President Carter was lying when he told the media that remote viewers had helped to locate a crashed Soviet spy plane. If he was telling the truth, then it was just a coincidence.

★ Erin Jones's dream about the Aberfan disaster was another coincidence. So were the 76 other premonitions that were investigated by a psychiatrist.

★ Ricardo Rossett must have simply been mistaken when he thought he saw Uri Geller bend a spanner, and so were the ten other witnesses in the pits at Silverstone when he did it.

★ D D Home was a skilled conjuror who easily tricked the respected scientist Sir William Crookes into wasting weeks of his life recording his paranormal feats. This included making one of the keenest minds of his age believe he had seen Home rise 18 inches off the ground before his very eyes.

★ Chico Xavier has obviously been employing a secret army of researchers and ghost-writers for nearly 70 years. He just memorises what they write and produces it at his public meetings. Then after going to all this trouble to trick people, he refuses to make any money out of his clever deception.

★ The Jesuit priest's diary of the Washington poltergeist case was a forgery. My book on the Enfield case was just another imaginative novel.

And so on. There will be those who believe some or all of these claims, like the White Queen in Alice Through the Looking-Glass could believe "as many as six impossible things before breakfast".

Dedicated sceptics can hold onto their old views even in the face of overwhelming evidence. To them, psi is simply taboo and not worth taking seriously. Here is Professor Peter Atkins of Oxford, holding forth in an interview he gave in 1998:

"Yes, I admit that I am prejudiced, if you like I'm a bigot and I have my mind closed to this kind of research. It's just a waste of time. Serious scientists have got real things to think about – we don't have time to waste on claims which we know both in our hearts and heads must be nonsense."

He added helpfully that, "I think there is no known effect that cannot be explained by conventional science."

Yet a careful look at the evidence, of which I could have included ten times as much if space had permitted, tells us that 'conventional science' must be open to change.

The same thing was true, of course, a century ago when the respected scientists of the day were telling us that X-rays, alternating current and powered flight were bunk. Indeed,

JUST A COINCIDENCE?

There has been fraud in psi research, to be sure, though nothing like as much as in 'straight' science in which there has certainly been enough to fill up many books.

In fact there have been only two major psi frauds. In one, researcher Walter Levy was caught fiddling the date by his colleagues and promptly shown the door. In the other, meticulous analysis revealed that S G Soal had also been altering his figures for a series of card-

Realities do not change, only the way we choose to look at them changes...

it has probably always been true, at least since the days when everybody knew that the Earth was flat and that the Sun went round it, or so everybody assumed. Realities do not change, only the way we choose to look at them changes.

guessing tests. As a recent survey has shown, however, the control conditions for psi experiments are stricter than they are in any other field of science.

Anyway, let us assume that one or two of the items on my list of impossible things might have been coincidences, and one or two involved fraud (although there is no evidence that any of them did). We are still left with quite enough to satisfy me, at least, that we are going to have to change our old ideas about such things as time, space and consciousness.

SHIFTING THE PARADIGMS

"We know," says the philosopher Max Payne, "that physical reality is far wider than the thin slice of it revealed by our five senses. Human experience is much higher, wider and deeper than official science allows us to describe. We require new paradigms of understanding."

A paradigm, in this context, means that set of beliefs and assumptions that determine how we look at things. At one time, there was no doubt that the Earth was at the centre of Creation, and everything else in the universe revolved around it. The Church said so and that was the end of the matter.

Then Copernicus and Kepler proved otherwise, and a new paradigm came into being. The Earth did not suddenly start spinning and going round the Sun. The universe did not change at all – it was the way we looked at it that changed.

Another massive paradigm shift took place in the 19th century, following Wallace and Darwin's shocking and revolutionary ideas of evolution, described by one commentator as proving that life was the result of "a purposeless and materialistic process".

A further shift took place early in the 20th century, when Einstein and others showed that the nice, solid and predictable physical world of the paradigm designed by Newton, was nothing of the kind. It had become a tangle of quantum indeterminacies, and collapsing wave-packets, hidden variables and Heaven knows what else.

MIND AND MATTER

Now, as we move into a new century, one of the biggest paradigm shifts of all time is well under way in which something relatively new has come into the picture: human consciousness. This in itself is not new, of course. What is new is that scientists have finally begun to take it seriously.

Some, like psi researcher Dean Radin, have gone so far as to suggest that "just as we were shocked to learn at the dawn of the 20th century that matter and energy were essentially the same, perhaps at the dawn of the 21st century we are about to discover that mind and matter are essentially the same?" As we shall see, there are many radical thinkers now who are starting to agree with this.

THE NETWORK EXPANDS

In 1973, a group of like-minded friends, including two senior government scientists, a university vice-chancellor and the head of a medical school, got together in order to found the Scientific and Medical Network. One of its main aims was to promote 'new paradigms of understanding', and it now has more than 2,000 members in 54 different countries.

Although, as its name would suggest, it is primarily a network of scientists and doctors, non-scientists can also become associates and attend regular meetings and conferences at which they can keep up to date with those new paradigms.

WHERE PSI IS HEADING

In April 1999 I went along to an all-day seminar devoted to theories of psi, at which several prominent Network members, including a Nobel laureate, gave us some idea of just how far paradigms have been shifting lately. Although the only thing I fully understood that day was my lunch, I did manage to get a sense of where psi research is heading.

One thing is quite clear – the old approach to science, which consists of taking things to

STARTING AGAIN

"Nature is complex and does not necessarily conform to the stereotypes we have had in the past," we were informed by Professor Brian Josephson, who won a Nobel prize for his ground-breaking work in solid-state electronics. The fact that he now heads something called

> The old approach to science, which consists in taking things to pieces, has given way to the 'holistic' view in which everything is considered to be connected...

pieces and studying them down to the last atom and beyond, has given way to the 'holistic' view in which everything, living or not, is considered to be directly connected to everything else. Universities may be divided into faculties and departments, but nature isn't.

the Mind-Matter Unification Project at Cambridge University is a sign of new times.

"We will have to start again and understand everything in terms of complex systems linked in ways that can't be explained by classical physics," he added, and admitted that we were still at the beginning of this particular shift in ideas, just as Newton was at the start of the one he set in motion. I was impressed by his humility, and struck by the contrast between his approach and that of his Cambridge colleague Stephen Hawking, according to whom we are coming close to the "theory of everything", the end of science and "reading the mind of God".

There is already a whole institute (in Santa Fe, New Mexico) devoted to the study of "the sciences of complexity" which is concerned with everything from the origins of life to the nature of the universe and where we fit into the great scheme of things.

This multi-disciplinary approach is very welcome, and the same approach must surely be taken to psi research. "Physicists can't go it alone," as one speaker reminded us.

All the same, it seems to me that they are the senior partners in this venture. They are the people who find out how things work, and they have been showing how psi phenomena are not as incompatible with the so-called laws of nature as we have been led to believe.

Physicists are now quite happy with such concepts as particles going backwards or forwards in time, and many more dimensions of space than we are able to conceive.

They have assured us, though not usually in simple language, that modern physics can already take on board the basic facts of psi: telepathy, clairvoyance, psychokinesis and precognition. These, as I hope I have made clear throughout this book, have now been proved to exist beyond reasonable doubt, yet definitely could not exist in terms of conventional science.

"When experience contradicts science, science must be changed", said Willis Harman, a former vice-president of the Network. And science is changing. It has yet to tell us how psi phenomena work, but it has admitted them to be possible.

It has also begun to sketch out the background in which they operate, and the picture that is now emerging is truly a mind-boggling one. "I regard the Self as being outside time and space", said Network veteran Geoffrey Latham. As he saw it, we are animated by an all-embracing sea of energy and consciousness. If this sounds too far out, let us remember that it was Einstein who said that the feeling that we are separated from the rest of the universe was "an optical illusion of consciousness" which in turn was "a kind of prison". It was our duty to escape from that prison, and at last we are starting to do so.

One who did manage to escape from it was Mary Craig Sinclair, whose own remarkable experiments, described in Chapter 1, led her to conclude that "we may be fountains or outlets of one vast mind".

We are animated by an all-embracing sea of energy and consciousness...

Psi researchers today are quite happy with the view that the mind is non-local, meaning that instead of being trapped in one body, it is actually present everywhere in both space and time. It is only our five senses that confine us to the here and now – if they didn't, we would be picking up everybody's thoughts all the time, which would be unbearable.

However, the evidence now suggests that under the right conditions and especially in an emergency, we are able to get through our own defences and link up directly with someone else's peace of mind.

SUPERMIND

And as for precognition, this becomes easier to understand if we are linked to a supermind located outside time and space as we know them. The same applies to the survival of physical death. If part of our selves can break through time and space barriers, as it can, then clearly it does not need a physical body and will survive the death of the one it happens to be occupying in this lifetime.

WILL FORCE

If all this is beginning to sound like the speculations of New Age nutters, it is worth remembering that similar ideas have been put forward before, and by scientists well grounded in reality. One who is frequently overlooked is Alfred Russell Wallace, the man who presented his theory of natural selection along with Charles Darwin's in 1858.

He never fully accepted that natural selection was the single driving force behind the process of evolution. He was especially puzzled by the fact that our primitive ancestors had brains which were far more highly developed than they needed to be. "Natural selection could only have endowed savage man with a brain a little superior to that of an ape," Wallace commented, "whereas he actually possessed one very little inferior to that of a philosopher."

So, he argued, "a superior intelligence has guided the development of man in a definite direction, and for a special purpose." He insisted that "some more general and fundamental law underlies that of natural selection." Nothing could be much further from Darwinism than this.

Wallace went on to make a speculation that was far ahead of its time. Writing about ten years before Einstein was born of any other primary cause of force, it does not seem an improbable conclusion that all force may be will-force: and thus that the whole universe is not merely dependent on – but actually is the WILL of higher intelligence or of one Supreme Intelligence."

> "All force may be will-force: and thus... the whole universe is not merely dependent on – but actually is the WILL of higher intelligence or of one Supreme Intelligence." – Alfred Wallace.

he noted that "matter is essentially force, and nothing but force" and it was clear that some force, at least, originated in the human mind. But where did the rest come from?

"If, therefore we have traced one force, however minute, to an origin in our own WILL, while we have no knowledge

Wallace was good at asking awkward questions. "Either all matter is conscious, or consciousness is something distinct from matter, and in the latter case, this presence in material forms is a proof of the existence of conscious beings outside of, and independent of, what we term matter." Each of us, he came to believe strongly, is "a duality, consisting of an organised spiritual form, evolved coincidentally with and permeating the physical body".

These were bold ideas for their time, when psi research had barely begun. Many of today's researchers would take them for granted.

MUCH BATTERING

Sadly, while paradigms shift sooner or later in science, there are always those like Richard Dawkins who cling to the old ones, and defend them to the last. To them, psi is simply taboo, and not worth taking seriously. Why not? Oh because there's no real evidence for it. Anway, it's impossible.

More than a century ago, Sir William Crookes – the scientist who investigated the medium Daniel Dunglas Home, and later went on to become president of the Royal Society –

faced similar attitudes, and recalled a friend who said: "the old wall of belief must be broken down by much battering".

The wall is giving in to the insistent battering here and there. You can now be referred to a healer on the National Health Service. You can study for a degree in parapsychology at several British universities. You can put your psi to work as part of your official duties in the US Army and be given a medal for your efforts.

Yet large parts of the old wall remain sturdily in their place. We batter on, convinced that eventually it will collapse into a pile of rubble, and be replaced by the 21st century paradigm. We look ahead to a time in which everything on our complex planet is finally recognised as being interconnected, and in which the human mind can at last begin to operate at its full power and potential.

FURTHER READING

Chapter 1
Andrija Puharich. Beyond Telepathy. 1962
Rupert Sheldrake. Seven Experiments That Could Change the World. 1994
Upton Sinclair. Mental Radio. 1930
Montague Ullman, S.Krippner & A.Vaughan. Dream Telepathy. (2nd ed.) 1989

Chapter 2
Joseph McMoneagle. Mind Trek.1993
Jim Schnabel. Remote Viewers. 1997
Russell Targ & Harold Puthoff. Mind-Reach. 1977

Chapter 3
J.W.Dunne. An Experiment with Time. 1927
J.B.Priestley. Man and Time. 1964
Dean Radin. The Conscious Universe. 1997
Russell Targ & Jane Katra. Miracles of Mind. 1998

Chapter 4
M.R.Barrington (ed.). Crookes and the Spirit World. 1972
Robert Jahn & Brenda Dunne. Margins of Reality. 1987
Guy Lyon-Playfair. Medicine, Mind & Magic. 1987
Charles Panati (ed.). The Geller Papers. 1976
Alfred Russell Wallace. Miracles and Modern Spiritualism. (2nd ed.) 1874

Chapter 5
A.H.Bell (ed.) Practical Dowsing. 1965 (Grattan)
Elmer & Alyce Green. Beyond Biofeedback. 1977
Bruce Macmanaway & Joanne Turcan. Healing. 1977
A.A.Mason. British Medical Journal, 23 August 1952.
Uri Geller & Guy Lyon-Playfair. The Geller Effect. 1986

CHAPTER 6
Anita Gregory. The Strange Case of Rudi Schneider. 1985
A.Imich (ed.) Incredible Tales of the Paranormal. 1995 (Kluski)

CHAPTER 7
Jule Eisenbud. The World of Ted Serios. 1968
Thelma Moss. The Body Electric. 1979
Guy Lyon-Playfair. The Indefinite Boundary. 1974 (Gasparetto)
Francisco Candido Xavier. Parnaso de Alem-Tumilo. 1932

CHAPTER 8
Jenny Cockell. Yesterday's Children. 1993
Joan Grant & Denys Kelsey. Many Lifetimes. 1970
Reincarnation International No 3, July 1994 (Pollock twins)
Jeffrey Iverson. In Search of the Dead. 1992
Paul Pearsall. The Heart's Code. 1998

CHAPTER 9
Thomas B.Allen. Possessed: The True Story of Exorcism. 1993
Counterblast. Where Scientists Fear to Tread. BBC2, 23 April 1998 (Atkins)
E.Gurney, F.W.H.Myers & F.Podmore. Phantasms of the Living. 1886. (Duthie)
D.Lorimer (ed.) Wider Horizons. 1999 (Sc.& Med. Network)
Guy Lyon-Playfair. This House is Haunted. 1980
Guy Lyon-Playfair. The Haunted Pub Guide. 1985
C.Neil-Smith. The Exorcist and the Possessed. 1974

USEFUL ADDRESSES

AMERICAN SOCIETY OF
PSYCHICAL RESEARCH
5 West 73rd Street
New York, NY 10023
U S A
www.aspr.com

ASSOCIATION FOR THE STUDY
OF ANOMALOUS PHENOMENA
(ASSAP)
20 Paul St.
Frome, Somerset BA11 1DX
http://dspace.dial.pipex.com/town/square/ee65

COLLEGE OF PSYCHIC STUDIES
16 Queensbury Place
London SW7 2EB

NATIONAL FEDERATION
OF SPIRITUAL HEALERS
Old Manor Farm Studio
Church St.
Sunbury-on-Thames,
Middlesex TW16 6RG
http://www.nfsh.org.uk

NOAH'S ARK SOCIETY
7 Sheen Close
Grange Park
Swindon, Wilts SN5 6JF
http://www.noahsark.clara.net

SCIENTIFIC & MEDICAL
NETWORK
Gibliston Mill
Colinsburgh
Leven, Fife KY9 1JS
http://www.cis.plym.ac.uk/SciMedNet
/home.htm

SCOTTISH SOCIETY FOR
PSYCHICAL RESEARCH
40 Highbury Road
Glasgow G12 8EF

SOCIETY FOR PSYCHICAL
RESEARCH
49 Marloes Road
London W8 6LA

SOCIETY OF SCIENTIFIC
EXPLORATION
PO Box 5848
Stanford, CA 94309-5848
U S A

URI GELLER WEBSITE
http://www.urigeller.com
http://www.tcom.co.uk/hpnet